ORCA ORIGINS TEACHER GUIDE

Building Empathy, Understanding and Knowledge

by Tasha Henry

ORCA BOOK PUBLISHERS

Explore Diversity

Orca Origins

with the Orca Origins

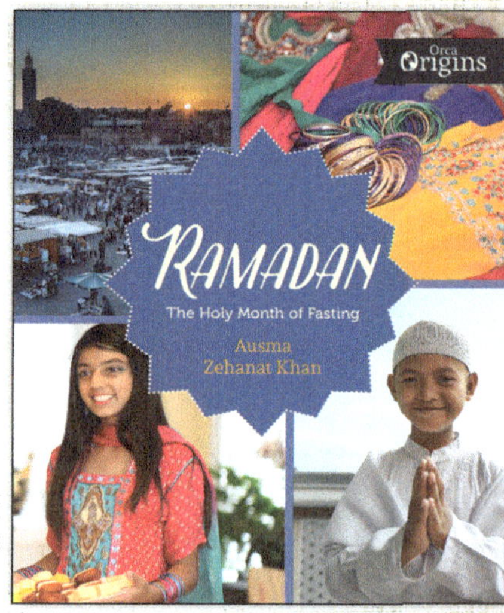

This teacher guide is a companion to the Orca Origins series for ages 9-12. To order the series, please visit **orcabook.com**.

Orca Book Publishers gratefully acknowledges the support for its publishing programs provided by the following agencies: the Government of Canada, the Canada Council for the Arts and the Province of British Columbia, and the Book Publishing Tax Credit.

ORCA BOOK PUBLISHERS
orcabook.com

Printed and bound in Canada.

22 21 20 19 • 4 3 2 1

ORCA ORIGINS TEACHER GUIDE

ORCA TEACHER RESOURCES

CONTENTS

INTRODUCTION

The Orca Origins series was developed to increase knowledge and awareness about significant cultural celebrations around the world. By looking at some of the world's beloved traditions, students will increase their understanding of the importance of cultural rituals and the people who celebrate them.

The celebrations of Ramadan, Passover, Diwali, Chinese New Year, Christmas and birthdays are presented through personal stories, narratives, recipes and reflections to emphasize that there are many different experiences even within each religion or belief system. By personalizing the ways in which communities and families celebrate, students will begin to understand that diversity lives in all beliefs and cultural practices around the world.

The content of this unit can encourage discussions and bring up questions that can be challenging for our learners. Since the historical roots of these celebrations touch on topics such as religion, immigration, racism, diaspora and cultural values, students may struggle with their own pre-conceived or previously learned ideas about people and culture. To support your students in their learning, a tone of empathy needs to be created and maintained throughout your class discussions and learning activities.

You will see that a common thread throughout this series is the theme of selflessness and generosity toward others, both locally and globally. As we research the origins and significance of these celebrations, we begin to see that the message of giving to those who are in need traverses cultural and religious differences. Finding daily classroom routines such as a morning circle, afternoon community cleanup or student-run clubs that support social justice can build community and forge a bond of togetherness that is essential to any learning about human compassion.

PLANNING YOUR SCHOOL YEAR AROUND CELEBRATION

Using This Guide

This teacher guide is organized into lesson sequences that offer suggested learning activities. These activities can be used in isolation, or you can use each one sequentially, chapter by chapter, depending on your time constraints. The guide presents the Origins books in a particular order that aligns with school-year celebrations. Many cultural celebrations and holidays are not included, but extra lessons or units can be added to better suit the needs of your classroom.

Consider engaging your class in thematic units of study and inquiry questions that reach beyond the classroom and encourage participation in the cultural events in your neighborhood. My hope is that with these learning activities, your students will bring a deepening knowledge to their participation in community events that are outside their own cultural practices. Knowledge is the springboard to empathy and compassion.

Check the exact dates of these cultural events (as they change every year) so that you can plan your units of study in conjunction with the families in your community who are already engaging in these festivities. Most of all, bring the outside world into your classroom through the rich and thoughtful exposure to these timeless celebrations around the globe.

Hopefully, by the end of each unit of study your class will have participated in the related cultural events in your school or community.

LEGEND

- Group Discussion
- Writing Activity
- Handout Available
- Research Activity
- Reading Activity

Getting Started

1. Have your students make a master list of all holidays, cultural events, harvests, festivals, etc., including birthdays. Ask your students to share their cultural backgrounds, if they know them, to contribute to the list of cultural celebrations.
2. Ask students to research the exact dates of the events in the current school year. For instance, Ramadan and Passover fall on different dates every year.
3. Build a school-year calendar using a template and upload it to your class website, use an app to upload the events, or print off a class calendar to post in the class.
4. Keeping in mind your climate, region and class makeup, ask your students to define some themes for the school based on the Origins books.

Suggested Sequence

September/October: Coming-of-Age Together
Birthdays: Beyond Cake and Ice Cream

November: Filling our Hearts with Light
Diwali: Festival of Lights

December: The Spirit of Giving
Christmas: From Solstice to Santa

January/February: Family and Community
Chinese New Year: A Celebration for Everyone

March/April: Gratitude
Passover: Festival of Freedom

May/June: Of Service to Others
Ramadan: They Holy Month of Fasting

Paper Bag Portfolio: Consider creating a paper-bag activity for the series. Before you begin each unit, give each student a paper bag and instruct them to decorate it and label it with the name of the cultural event being studied. They will choose five objects to place inside the bag to represent their learning. These could be artifacts or keepsakes from home, a souvenir from an event or a written reflection. For instance, a candle could be placed in the Diwali paper bag to represent the candles lit to celebrate this festival of light. Or the artifacts could be drawings of an object or symbol that represents the student's understanding of the cultural celebration. Have students present their artifacts in small groups to express their understanding and their personal connections to the celebration they studied.

BIRTHDAYS: BEYOND CAKE AND ICE CREAM
BY NIKKI TATE AND DANI TATE-STRATTON

Big Idea

For centuries, people around the world have honored and celebrated birthdays in many different ways. Rites of passage are practiced by cultures all over the world to commemorate an individual's development and their place in community.

Unit Guiding Questions

- What community rituals do we take for granted today around celebrating birthdays?
- How did our ancestors celebrate birthdays?
- How do cultures around the world celebrate?

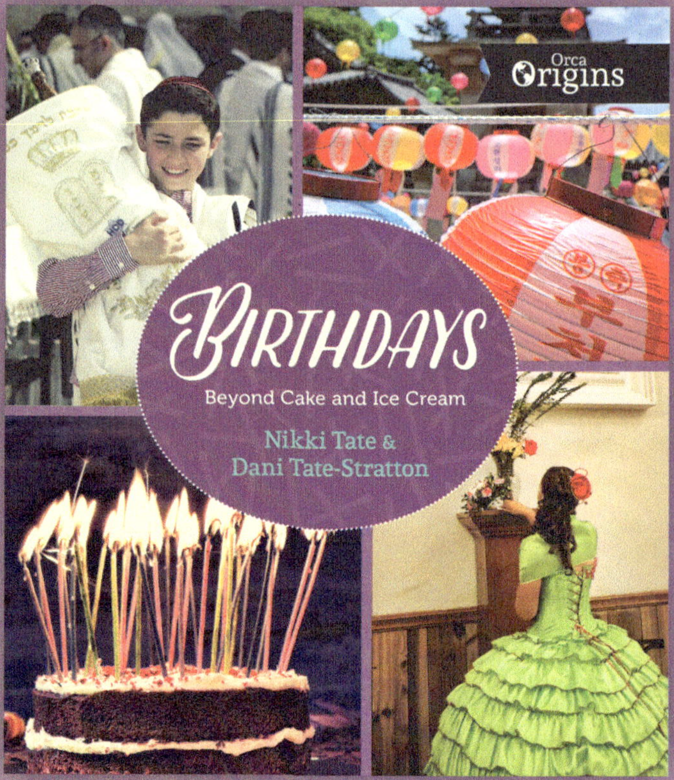

Introduction

1. Ask your students to decide how they would like to celebrate or honor their classmates on their special day. Some may want to celebrate on their birthdays. Some parents may want to send baked goods on their child's birthday. Other children may not know how or even whether they want to be honored in the classroom setting. Here are some ideas:
    a. Make a friendship fan. Fold a piece of card stock into a fan. Pass the fan around and have each child write a positive or encouraging word or phrase on one section of the fan for the child they are honoring. The child can keep it private, or it can be displayed in the room, adding to the display each time a fan is made for another student.
    b. Paint rocks with uplifting, celebratory words or phrases. On the day the child is honored, they get a painted rock letting them know how special they are.
    c. Have a community circle or a check-in circle where the class focuses on the child whose birthday they are celebrating. Have each student say one positive thing about that child. Close the circle by sharing food or by giving a symbol of the circle to the child (a card or trinket). *Note: Not all children love their birthdays. Birthdays can be painful times for children who are separated from loved ones or whose religion does not celebrate birthdays. Be aware of the unique needs of your classroom, and accommodate as necessary.*
2. After reading the introduction, ask your students what conditions may make birthdays a difficult time for some people. Reference how not all children celebrate their birthdays as a special event. Emphasize that the classroom, as a community, can celebrate rites of passage in the ways they see fit.

Chapter One: The Birth of Birthdays

1. Have students complete the "*Birthdays:* Chapter One Comprehension Questions" handout after reading the chapter.
2. Have students read the "Party Like an Egyptian" section (pages 11–15), including the "Birthday Treats" sidebar and the captions under the images, and then write down on strips of paper three interesting facts. Put the interesting facts in a bowl and pass it around. Have each student pick a fact and read it to the class.
3. Have each student complete the goal-setting instructions in "Give It a Whirl" (page 19) and put the finished responses in a sealed envelope. Keep the envelopes in a safe place until the end of the school year. Students

can then read their reflections and see how much they've grown since the beginning of the year.

4. Have students work on their own or in pairs and look up the meaning of the vocabulary words in bold in the glossary (page 73). Students can then create a word-search puzzle (and answer key) using ten or more words. Have students trade crosswords and then complete them.
5. Have students choose one of the two research activities:
   a. Research UNICEF's international rights of the child. Write a simple, informative pamphlet about a child's rights and how unregistered births can affect these rights. Include reasons why these rights exist, how many births are unregistered according to UNICEF and why parents would not want or be able to register a child's birth. Remember to reference your sources.
   b. Research ten important figures from different parts of the world whose birthdays are recognized as national holidays. Write a simple, informative pamphlet about the historical background of each of these figures, including their legacy and the reason their birthday is significant to that country. In your conclusion, recommend one person from your homeland, community or country whose birthday should be recognized as a national holiday. Convince your audience of your opinion with concrete ways this individual has contributed to society.

Chapter Two: Celebrating Birthdays around the World

Have students read this chapter, then use the **"Birthday Traditions around the World"** handout to try to remember the different ways people celebrate each passing year with specific foods and birthday rituals.

Chapter Three: Milestone Birthdays

Be an Anthropologist!

An anthropologist is someone who researches people from the past and present and studies their culture, traditions and values. After reading this chapter, your students will realize that different cultures mark rites of passage and comings-of-age in different ways. Have your students research three different coming-of-age rituals in three distinct cultures and do a cross-cultural analysis of the similarities and differences they found. Have your students present their findings with a report, video, poster or a medium of their choosing. Your students can use the **"Be an Anthropologist Assessment Checklist"** handout to check their project's quality.

a. Informative report: Use pictures, illustrations or diagrams to describe the research. Write in complete sentences. Include works cited.
b. Video: Use appropriate music and images that capture the research. Include works cited.
c. Research poster: Use graphics and images to support the research. Write in point form. Include works cited.

Piñatas are often made from papier-mâché but can also be created from pottery or cloth.

Cathy Yeulet/iStock.com

DIWALI: FESTIVAL OF LIGHTS
BY RINA SINGH

Big Idea

Diwali is a Hindu festival of light that represents the triumph of light over dark, or good over evil. Diwali has changed as South Asians have emigrated from their home countries.

Unit Guiding Questions

- What are the Hindu legends that inspired Diwali?
- How has Diwali changed with the people around the world who celebrate it?
- How have consumerism and capitalism changed the celebration of Diwali?
- What are the pros and cons of modernizing traditional holidays like Diwali around the world?

Introduction

1. Together as a class, flip through the whole book, looking only at the pictures and recipes. Ask your students which images jump out at them. Ask if any of your students have celebrated Diwali. What are their favorite memories of or experiences with this celebration? Can they find pictures in the book that remind them of their own celebration? What do these images tell them about Indian culture? Which recipe looks most appetizing to them? Are there any ingredients that surprise them?
2. Have students find the "Diwali Facts" throughout the book. Write down the facts on the board or a large piece of paper. Ask your students what surprises them about each fact. What does this fact make them wonder about?
3. Have students read the introduction and complete the **"*Diwali:* Introduction Comprehension Questions"** handout.

Chapter One: What is Diwali?

1. Ask your students to think about a time when their senses were overwhelmed with colors, sounds, tastes and sights. Where were they? How did it feel? Have your students share a memory with a partner.
2. Have your students read the chapter and note things that jump out at them, using the **"Four Things Chart"** handout to record their thoughts.

Chapter Two: The History of Indian Immigration

1. Write the terms *South Asian*, *East Indian*, *Indian*, *West Indian* on the board and ask your students if they know the difference between these terms. Introduce the concept of a *denonym* (a name for people that derives from geographical origins). For example, *Canadian* is a denonym, as it refers to people from Canada. *Indian* is a denonym, as it refers to people of India. Have your students list countries where the people of that country are referred to by a denonym. Describe the colonial history of the usage of the term *Indian*. European colonizers called people from India "East Indians" to distinguish them from the Native "Indians," or Indigenous Peoples of North and South America. When Columbus ran into the Caribbean islands on his way to the Indian subcontinent, he called the people there "West Indians" to distinguish them from the "East Indians," or the people from India.
2. Explain that the common and more widely accepted term for people from India is South Asian, which includes the nations of India, Pakistan,

Bangladesh, Nepal, Bhutan, Maldives and Sri Lanka. Have students shade and label the countries in South Asia and the West Indies, signifying them with different colors using the "World Map" handout.

3. Have students complete the "*Diwali:* Chapter Two Comprehension Questions" handout after reading the chapter.

Chapter Three: The Evolution of Diwali

Read the chapter together. On page 58, the author talks about how often children of immigrants are "caught between two cultures" and "learn to balance the two cultures." Ask your students to analyze these quotes. Have your students draw a picture or make a collage from magazines using images and words that expresses what it feels like to have one foot in two worlds. These two worlds could be cultural, as expressed by the author and in "Sapna's Story" (pages 62–63), or they could be economic worlds, social worlds or any two worlds that divide our identity and challenge us to bridge two belief systems. Ask students to present their pictures or collages to the class.

Chapter Four: Diwali around the World

As you read the chapter, have your students think about commonalities and differences in how Diwali is celebrated outside of India. On the board or a large sheet of paper, use a series of Venn diagrams or a web to record the differences and similarities between celebrations in Nepal, Great Britain, Singapore, Thailand, South Africa, Suriname and Trinidad and the celebrations in India.

Be a Travel Writer!

A travel writer is someone who writes about countries around the world to make readers want to go on vacation there. After reading chapter 4, your students will understand the history of Diwali and how it is celebrated around the world. Have your students write an article for a travel magazine about the celebration of Diwali and what travelers preparing for a trip to India during Diwali should expect. The article must define the meaning of Diwali and include an overview of the differences between Hindu, Sikh, Jain and Islam cultures. The article should use images such as maps, photos or drawings to give information to its readers. Your students can use the "Be a Travel Writer Assessment Checklist" handout to check their project's quality.

CHRISTMAS: FROM SOLSTICE TO SANTA
BY NIKKI TATE AND DANI TATE-STRATTON

Big Idea

People from different parts of the world celebrate Christmas in different ways. From Egyptian to Ancient Roman and Greek to Celtic traditions, midwinter festivals have been celebrated for centuries.

Unit Guiding Questions

- What are the known origins of winter solstice celebrations?
- How did the spread of Christianity affect the Christmas celebration?
- How has commercialism affected Christmas?

Introduction

Have your students write about a memory or a tradition they celebrate at this time of year. Include things like certain foods or events they have experienced. Together as a class, have students explain the memory or tradition they wrote about. Write down the different traditions on the board or a large piece of paper. Discuss the similarities and differences between the different traditions. You can go back to this list throughout the unit and discuss the history of some of these traditions.

Chapter One: Season of Darkness, Season of Light

1. After your students have read the chapter, ask them to complete the "*Christmas:* Chapter One Comprehension Questions" handout. This can be done as they read or with a partner after reading the chapter.
2. Have your students complete the "Midwinter Traditions Scavenger Hunt" handout.
3. After reading pages 15–25, have students complete the "*Christmas:* Matching Activity" handout in small groups or individually. After the unit you can use the same handout to assess retention of the concepts presented in this chapter.

Chapter Two: The Beginnings of Modern Christmas

1. As your students read the chapter, have them use the "KWL Chart" handout to explain the roots of Santa Claus, Christmas music, Christmas trees and gift giving during the Christmas celebration with references to the information in the book. Use images or pictures in the boxes if appropriate.
2. Have your students read the personal stories: Colin's Story, Nikki's Story, Dani's Story, Dani's German Christmases, Renata's Story. Discuss as a class any common themes. Ask your students to think about special times—wonderful meals or family rituals or occasions that have filled them with the spirit of giving. Ask your students to write a one-page memoir about a family occasion that brought them joy.

Chapter Three: Celebrations around the World

Have your students write an opinion piece about how consumerism has affected the celebration of Christmas around the globe. Your students should consider how marketing has employed the stories of Christmas to affect how people choose to give during this holiday and the roots of the rituals associated with giving around Christmas in the context of consumer movements in North America.

Be a Detective!

A detective is someone who investigates a mystery by collecting information or clues. After reading this chapter, your students will understand the history of Christmas and how it is celebrated around the world. Have your students choose a symbol of Christmas (it could be a food, a character or a carol) and investigate its roots. They should find out how the symbol adapted over time, what it represents now, how cultural symbols work and how symbols are affected by the people who reference them. Have your students present their findings in a report, slide-show presentation, poster or another medium of their choosing. Together as a class, create an assessment checklist so your students can check their project's quality.

a. Informative report: Use pictures, illustrations or diagrams to describe the research. Write in complete sentences. Include works cited.

b. Slide-show presentation: Use graphics and images to support the research. Write in point form. Include works cited.

c. Research poster: Use graphics and images to support the research. Write in point form. Include works cited.

Some people say that Santa keeps two lists of children's names—one for naughty girls and boys, and one for nice children.

lisegagne/iStock.com

CHINESE NEW YEAR: A CELEBRATION FOR EVERYONE
BY JEN SOOKFONG LEE

Big Idea

Chinese New Year is celebrated by multicultural and diverse communities across the globe. Chinese New Year celebrations have changed over time and differ with the cultures who celebrate it. Some of the reasons people of all backgrounds enjoy the festivities of Chinese New Year every year are diaspora and the human need to preserve traditions and community cultural values.

Unit Guiding Question

- What are the origins of Chinese New Year and how has this celebration adapted to the Chinese diaspora around the globe?

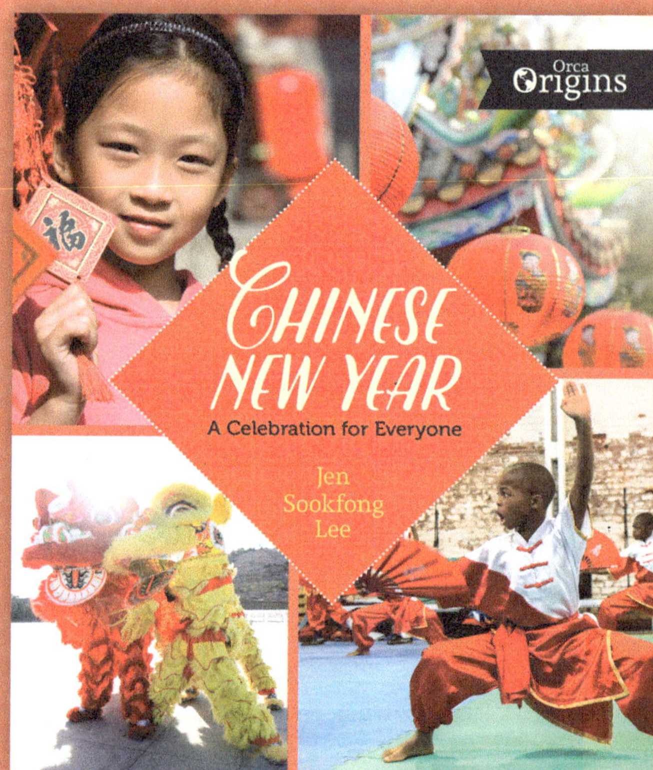

Introduction

Read the introduction out loud to the class. Have your students complete the **"Sensory Poem Writing Activity"** handout.

Chapter One: What Chinese New Year Is All About

1. After your students have read the chapter, ask them to complete the **"*Chinese New Year:* Chapter One Comprehension Questions"** handout.
2. Explain that *homophones* are words that sound the same but have different spellings and meanings. Using the author's story in the "CNY Facts" section on page 20, find examples of homophones and print them on the board. Have students pair up and take turns putting each word in a sentence and thinking of more homophones to add to the list. Using the **"Homophone Bingo"** handout, have students pick eight words from the list and print them on their bingo cards. Read out the words in random order, being sure to put them in a sentence. Once someone calls out, "Bingo," your students can trade cards and start again.

Chapter Two: How Chinese New Year Spread around the World

1. Read the chapter out loud as a class. Ask your students to explain what *filial piety* means in Chinese culture and think of examples of these values in other cultures.
2. Have your students imagine what it would be like to be a Chinese immigrant moving to Canada or the United States around the year 1900. Have your students write a letter to their family back in China, using the information in the chapter or doing further research on the experiences of Chinese immigrants to inform the historical data of their letter. Your students can use the **"Letter from the Past Self-Assessment Checklist"** handout to check the quality of their writing.

Chapter Three: How Chinese New Year Is Celebrated Today

1. After your students have read the chapter, ask them to complete the **"*Chinese New Year:* Chapter Three Comprehension Questions"** handout.
2. Have your students go through the chapter and write down ten true-or-false questions on sticky notes or pieces of paper. This can be done individually or in small groups. Your students should have five questions for which the answer is true and five for which the answer is false. Using the

"Fact Sort Activity" handout, have your students trade questions and sort answers into the true and false columns. You can do several rounds of this game to assess their comprehension of this section of the book.

Chapter Four: Chinese New Year Celebrations across the Globe

Explain that *diaspora* means the dispersion of a cultural group from its original homeland. As you read the chapter together as a class, use the following questions to further class discussion.

1. What realization did the author have after researching and writing this book?
2. How has immigration strengthened Chinese cultural traditions? How has it posed cultural challenges? Name a few mentioned in the chapter.
3. What is the difference between emigration and immigration?
4. How do cultural traditions help shape identity?
5. How do cultural celebrations shape community?
6. What is the connection between personal and social responsibility when it comes to learning about cultures other than your own?

Be a Graphic Designer!

A graphic designer is someone who creates posters, billboards, brochures or ads that provide people with information in a visual way. After reading this chapter, your students will understand the history of Chinese New Year and how it is celebrated around the world. Have your students create a collage or pop-up poster to tell people about a Chinese New Year celebration. Your students should use at least five different images that represent the values and meaning of Chinese New Year and then research and define what these images symbolize.

iStock.com/yipengge

PASSOVER: FESTIVAL OF FREEDOM

BY MONIQUE POLAK

Big Idea

The Passover story encourages all people to overcome obstacles, stand up for others, and acknowledge that everyone should be free to practice their religion without persecution.

Unit Guiding Questions

- How has the Holocaust affected the tradition of Passover?
- How does the symbolism of the Passover seder speak to Jewish history?
- How does altruism play a part in this Jewish celebration?

Introduction

1. Before reading the introduction together as a class, create a KWL chart on either the board or a large piece of paper. Ask your students what they know about Passover and what they would like to learn throughout the unit. If there are any Jewish class members, they may want to share their experiences of celebrating Passover.
2. Have your students read the introduction individually and write down any words that are in bold. Once they have finished reading the chapter, have them go to the glossary at the back of the book and record the definitions of the words.
3. Have students color and cut a hamsa amulet using the "Hamsa Amulet Decoration" handout and hang it in your classroom.

Chapter One: What's Passover All About?

1. Have your students read all of the chapter except for "Ben's Story (Part One)" individually or in small groups. As they are reading, have them write down the key events of the Israelites' escape from Egypt. Using these key points, have your students draw a comic using the "*Passover:* Comic Storyboard" handout.
2. Ask students to define the meaning of a symbol. Have your students find out what each food on a traditional seder plate symbolizes, using the "Seder Meal Symbols" handout.
3. Read "Ben's Story (Part One)" aloud to the whole class. Ask your students to remember a time when they shared food or a meal with loved ones. Ask them to conjure the smell of that food. Have your students use the "Symbol Poem Writing Activity" handout to create a symbol poem using this memory as a guide.

Chapter Two: Passover before and after the Holocaust

1. Different classes will have had different exposure to this time in history. Ask your students to tell you what they already know about the Holocaust. You will have to gauge how in-depth you want to go into this unit of study. Ask your school librarian for some good resources, books or short, age-appropriate films about the Holocaust.
2. After your students have read the chapter, ask them to complete the "*Passover:* Chapter Two Comprehension Questions" handout.

3. Read "Ben's Story (Part Two)" and "Liselotte's Story" aloud to the class. This could take several days. Be prepared for your kids to ask difficult questions about the Holocaust. Liselotte explains that she sews quilts for a women's shelter in her free time. Together as a class, construct a classroom freedom quilt. Give each student a square of either paper or plain fabric to draw what freedom means to them or what reading Ben and Liselotte's stories made them feel. Attach the squares together and display the quilt somewhere in the classroom.
4. Have your students write a letter to Ben or Liselotte to thank them for sharing their story.

Chapter Three: Passover in Action

1. Read the chapter together as a class. Ask your students what they think altruism is and to name different ways that kids are doing *tzedakah*.
2. Divide your students into small groups. Have a role for each member in the group (e.g., interviewer, recorder, tech person, etc.). Each group will research one of the organizations referred to in the book or find a local organization that does similar work. Have the groups create ten interview questions for a staff member at the chosen organization. Have the students interview that person about the organization, either in person, over the phone or via email. After the interviews are complete, have the groups present their findings to the class.

Chapter Four: Passover around the World

Be a Cultural Ambassador!

A cultural ambassador is someone who represents their culture in another country. After reading this chapter, your students will understand the history of Passover and how it is celebrated around the world. Divide your students into the six "home" groups:

a. Europe: The Netherlands, Italy, Ukraine
b. Israel
c. China and Nepal
d. Ethiopia
e. Iraq
f. Morocco

Have each home group create notes on cards about how they celebrate Passover in their region, by reading the chapter or doing extra research. Create new groups so that one person from each home group goes to a mixed group. They are now cultural ambassadors for their home group. Have each student describe how Passover is celebrated in their home group. In the mixed groups, have your students write down how the different home groups celebrate. Go around the class and ask each student to share one or two things they learned in their mixed group.

Father prepares son for prayer at the Western Wall.
Gosiek-B/iStock.com

RAMADAN: THE HOLY MONTH OF FASTING

BY AUSMA ZEHANAT KHAN

Big Idea

Ramadan is a Muslim tradition that is celebrated around the world. It values respect, self-discipline, gratitude and giving. At the heart of this Islamic tradition is the intention to help those in need.

Unit Guiding Questions

- What is the purpose behind the Ramadan tradition?
- What are the tenets, beliefs and traditions at the root of this celebration?

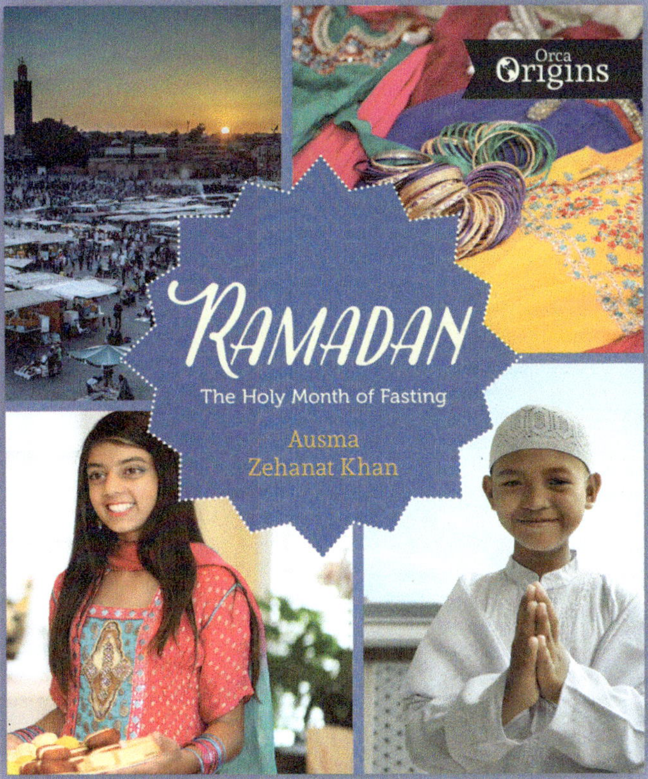

Introduction

1. Have your students flip through the book and read the colorful speech bubbles that describe what Ramadan means to some of the kids who celebrate it. Ask students to write about what they think is a common idea or feature in these speech bubbles and how they can relate it to their own lives.
2. Read the introduction together as a class. Ask your students if they can think of a time when they didn't tell a friend about something important in their life. What feelings prevented them from sharing with that friend? Why did Ausma feel guilty?

Chapter One: What Is Ramadan?

1. After your students have read the chapter, ask them to complete the "*Ramadan:* Chapter One Comprehension Questions" handout.
2. Have your students go through the chapter and write down ten true-or-false questions on sticky notes or pieces of paper. This can be done individually or in small groups. Your students should have five questions for which the answer is true and five for which the answer is false. Using the "Fact Sort Activity" handout, have your students trade questions and sort answers into the true and false columns. Alternatively, if you have limited time or your students are struggling with creating their own questions and need additional scaffolding, you can have your students complete the activity using the "*Ramadan:* Fact Sort Activity" handout with premade questions.

Chapter Two: The Stages of Ramadan

1. After students have read the chapter, ask them to complete the "Ramadan: Chapter Two Comprehension Questions" handout.
2. Have students choose one of the reflective writing prompts to complete.
    a. Read Layth's quote on page 37. What is self-discipline? Have you had an experience where you faced a challenge and had to be disciplined in your approach to this challenge? What did you learn from this experience?
    b. Read Hamzah's story on page 44. What is funny about Hamzah's story? How do you know that Hamzah is a good friend? Can you think of a time when you accidentally brought attention to yourself? How did you recover from the situation?

Chapter Three: The Spirit of Ramadan

After students have read the chapter, ask them to complete the **"Spirit of Ramadan Research Activity"** handout.

Chapter Four: Ramadan Traditions around the World

Be a Journalist!

A journalist is someone who researches and writes articles about interesting topics, such as recent events. After reading this chapter, your students will understand the history of Ramadan and how it is celebrated around the world. Have your students research Ramadan traditions from three different countries and write a compare-and-contrast essay that describes the similarities and differences between different traditions. Your students can use the **"Ramadan Essay Template"** handout to help them write their rough draft.

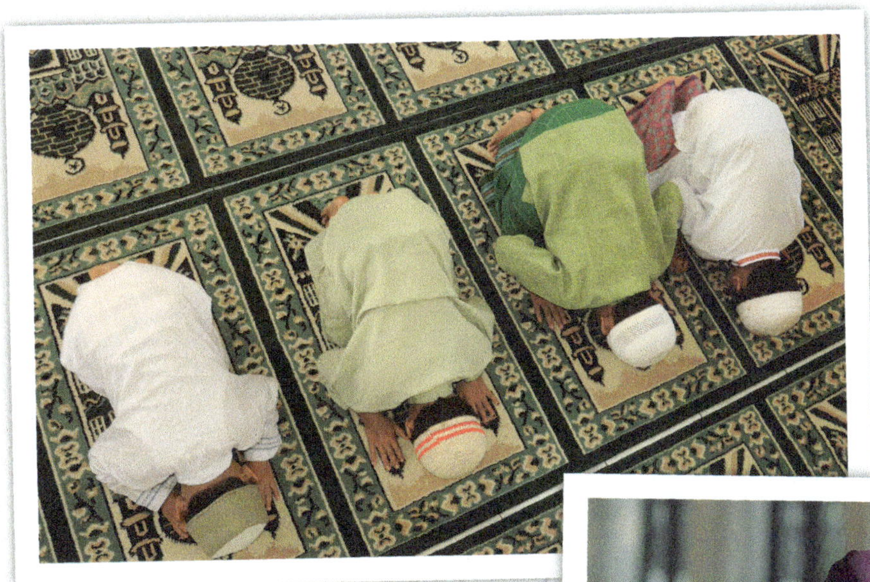

Muslim boys prostrate in prayer.
iStock.com/DistinctiveImages

Muslim girls study their faith.
iStock.com/Yamtono_Sardi

Conclusion to Orca Origins Unit

1. Have your students write a culminating compare-and-contrast essay about three major celebrations around the world. Your students can use the "Essay Template" handout to help with their rough draft.
2. Have a cultural celebration day with the class. Use projects created throughout the year, such as the classroom freedom quilt from the Passover unit and the posters from the Chinese New Year unit, to decorate the room. Pick a few of the recipes in the book. Is it possible to make one in your class or at home, or have students bring in their favorite foods from their culture? Ask if any parents or someone from your community can come into your class to show you how to prepare a traditional food. Ask if any of your students have a dance, a traditional outfit or another part of their culture that they would like to share with the class.

From *Christmas: From Solstice to Santa.*
iStock.com

HANDOUTS AND ASSESSMENT TOOLS

FATCAMERA/ISTOCK.COM

TEACHER RESOURCES

Birthdays:
Chapter One Comprehension Questions

Name: ______________________________

1. Who were the first people to develop a calendar?

___

2. What ancient practice informed every aspect of life in Ancient Egypt and Ancient China?

___

3. In what book is the first mention of a birthday?

___

4. Why did Romans wait until nine days after a baby was born before they celebrated the "day of purification"?

___

5. Who were the first known peoples to celebrate birthdays other than those of gods and goddesses? Whose birthdays were not celebrated?

___

6. Whose birthday was marked by the first known symbol of a cake with candles? What did it represent?

___

7. Why were birthdays not celebrated during the early Middle Ages?

___

8. Define the Renaissance.

___

9. Define the Industrial Revolution.

___

10. Who was Jawaharlal Nehru? Why is his birthday celebrated as "Children's Day"?

___

11. Which of the following people does ***not*** have a national holiday in their country on their birthday? George Washington, Buddha, Martin Luther King, Queen Victoria, Nelson Mandela, Jesus Christ, Jawaharla Nehru.

___

ORCA TEACHER RESOURCES

Birthdays: Birthday Traditions around the World

Name: ______________________

COUNTRY OR REGION	TYPES OF FOOD	ACTIVITIES/RITUALS
United States—Winnebago tribe		
Nigeria		
Germany		
Egypt		
Philippines		
Norway		
India		
Ecuador		
Israel		

Orca Book Publisher © 2019 Orca Origins Teacher Guide by Tasha Henry • ISBN 9781459822443

Be an Anthropologist Assessment Checklist

Name: ______________________

Use this chart for self-assessment, peer assessment and teacher evaluation.

	I need more (I haven't included enough yet)	Somewhat (My work lacks some detail)	Yes! (I have met the criteria)
I referenced three cultures thoroughly			
I used images to support my research			
I analyzed the similarities and differences of these cultures without giving my opinion			
I used data, details and historical information to thoroughly describe the similarities and differences			
I have concluded with a statement about why coming-of-age rituals span cultures			
I have referenced my sources accurately			
I have successfully used my medium to represent my research			

Diwali:
Introduction Comprehension Questions

Name: ______________________________

1. What does the word Diwali mean in Sanskrit?

___

2. What is a monotheistic religion?

___

3. Is Hinduism a monotheistic religion? Why or why not?

___

___

4. Is Sikhism a monotheistic religion? Why or why not?

___

___

5. Who is the Hindu goddess of wealth?

___

6. Why did the author feel grateful when she was asked to write this book?

___

___

Four Things Chart

Name: ______________________________

Four things that surprised me	Four things that confused me	Four things that I want to learn more about	Four things that inspired me

Orca Book Publisher © 2019 Orca Origins Teacher Guide by Tasha Henry • ISBN 9781459822443

World Map

Name: ____________________

Diwali: Chapter Two Comprehension Questions

Name: ____________________

1. Which people were excluded from coming to the United States in 1882?

2. What law was passed in 1917?

3. How were people from India described before 1965 in the census records?

4. Why, by the 1980s, were there more than 400,000 Indians living in the United States?

5. Who were the first people from India to arrive in Canada? In what year?

6. What is the example of the racial slur that Sikhs experienced in Canada?

7. Complete the timeline of immigration of South Asian people coming to Canada.

Year	Description of incident, act or policy in Canada
1897	
1903	
1906	
1907	
1908	
1913	
1914	
2016	

Diwali: Chapter Two Comprehension Questions (cont.)

Name: ______________________________

8. What feelings, thoughts and impressions are you left with after reading this chapter? Can you see evidence that attitudes toward immigrants have changed in Canada or the United States? Why or why not? Write about your thoughts and offer some solutions.

9. Read "Swati's Story" on pages 40–41. What does it mean to you when she says, "To me, it sounds like an America where there is room for all of us"? How has immigration strengthened new countries like Canada and the United States?

Orca Book Publisher © 2019 Orca Origins Teacher Guide by Tasha Henry • ISBN 9781459822443

Be a Travel Writer Assessment Checklist

Name: ____________________

Use this chart for self-assessment, peer assessment and teacher evaluation.

	I need more (I haven't included enough yet)	Somewhat (My work lacks some detail)	Yes! (I have met the criteria)
I have information about the four major religions in India.			
I have information about the history and origins of Diwali.			
I encouraged my readers to experience India's diverse culture.			
I have appropriate images to support my information.			
My writing recognizes my audience (people traveling to India).			
My writing uses proper spelling, punctuation and grammar.			
My writing suits the form of a magazine article.			

Christmas: Chapter One Comprehension Questions

Name: ______________________________

1. Why do hot countries or tropical countries have a "midwinter" celebration?

2. What is the date of the shortest day of the year in the northern hemisphere?

3. How is the sun connected to this midwinter celebration?

4. What is the significance of the yule log?

5. What are some logical reasons why midwinter celebrations have survived for thousands of years?

6. Describe the ancient Roman celebration Saturnalia.

7. Explain the rituals in Ancient Greece in midwinter.

8. Read the sidebar on page 13. What is the reason for Boxing Day? How is this holiday interpreted today?

Midwinter Traditions Scavenger Hunt

Name: ______________________________

In point form, fill in where these different midwinter traditions started. Draw a picture or write a description of each tradition. Remember to read the captions and text boxes too.

Traditions	Place	Drawing or Description
Yule Logs and the Yule Goat		
Boxing Day		
Flying Chariots		
Christmas Carols		
Saint Nicholas		

ORCA TEACHER RESOURCES

Christmas:
Matching Activity

Name: ____________________

Cut out the different words at the bottom of the page and glue them next to the matching definition.

1. The Dutch name for St. Nicholas ____________________
2. Known to Christians as the three kings or three wise men ____________________
3. A miniature nativity scene ____________________
4. A resin from trees grown in the Middle East ____________________
5. A religion that believes in the life and teachings of a Jewish prophet names Jesus Christ ____________________
6. Roman sun god ____________________
7. The time the Roman Empire adopted Christianity as the main religion ____________________
8. Composed one of the first known Christmas Carols in the fourth century CE ____________________
9. Part of the Bible that was written by different authors during the first century CE ____________________
10. Christ's Mass or the feast of Nativity ____________________
11. The days between Christmas and Epiphany ____________________
12. Before the Common Era ____________________
13. Symbolizes everlasting life ____________________
14. Group of Protestant Christians who banned Christmas ____________________

Vocabulary Words

Puritans	Advent wreath	New Testament	Christmas
Sinterklaas	BCE	Sol Invictus	Crèche
Magi	fourth century in Rome	St. Hilary of Poitiers	
12 days of Christmas	Myrrh	Christianity	

KWL Chart: Thinking Clouds

Name: ______________________________

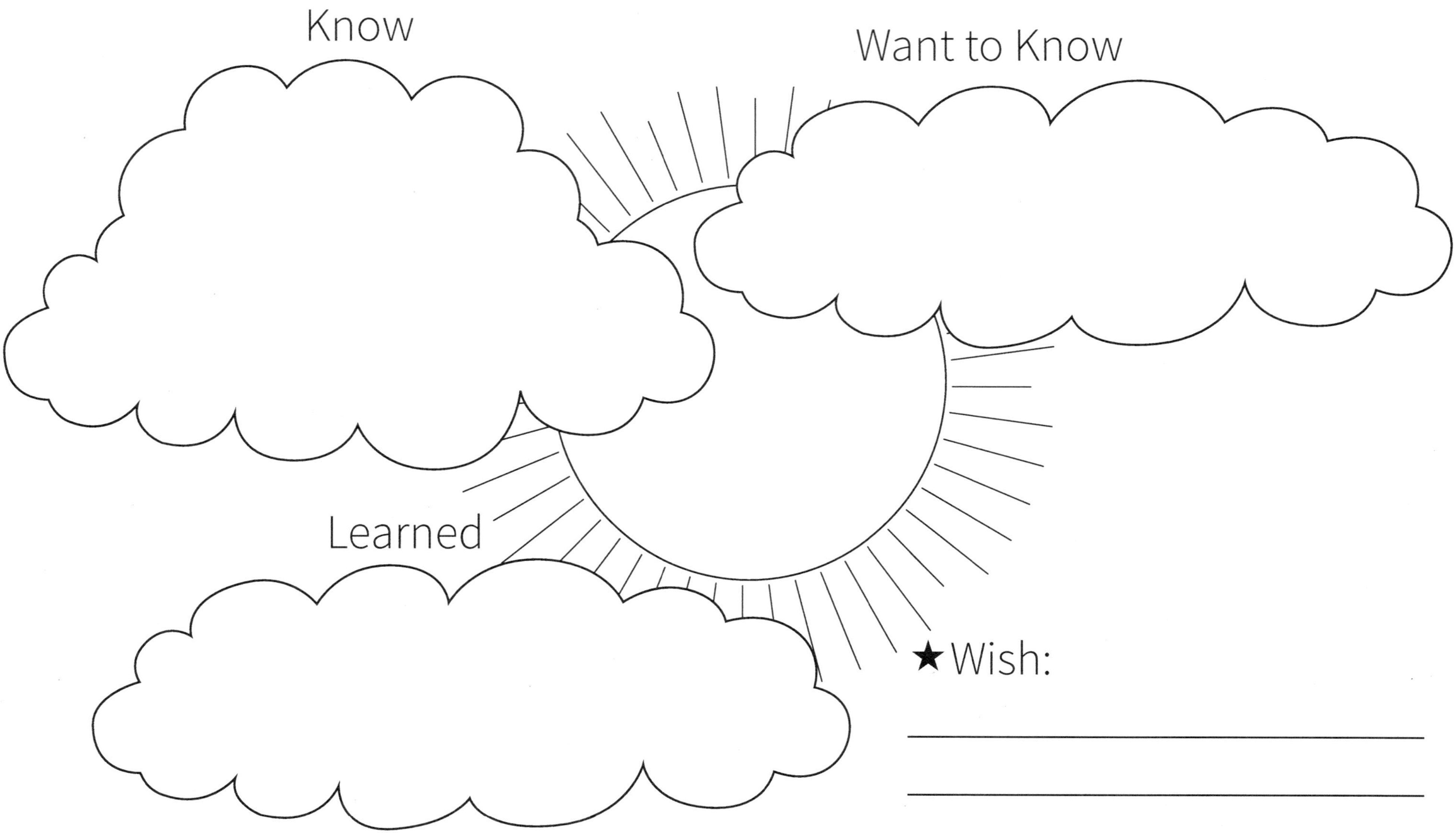

★ Wish:

____

____

____

Orca Book Publisher © 2019 Orca Origins Teacher Guide by Tasha Henry • ISBN 9781459822443

Sensory Poem Writing Activity

ORCA TEACHER RESOURCES

Name: ______________________________

Have you visited or do you live in a city that has a Chinatown? What colors, textures and smells do you remember from that visit? Did you attend a Chinese New Year parade or Spring Festival?

Think of your first memory of Chinatown or refer to Jen's story about Vancouver's Chinatown. Use the poem template to describe all the senses and help you write your sense poem.

I smell ______________________________ .

I hear ______________________________ .

I feel ______________________________ .

I taste ______________________________ .

I see ______________________________ .

Cut and paste an image or draw an abstract image that captures the feeling of this poem.

Orca Book Publisher © 2019 Orca Origins Teacher Guide by Tasha Henry • ISBN 9781459822443

Chinese New Year: Chapter One Comprehension Questions

Name: ______________________________

1. Chinese New Year is also known as ______________________________
2. According to the legend of Nián, why have the color red and the loud sounds of the fire-crackers become part of the Chinese New Year celebration? ______________________________
3. According to legend, why is each lunar calendar year signified by an animal? Look at the chart on page 17 and find your birth year. What animal in the Chinese zodiac are you? What qualities are associated with this animal? Do you agree with these attributes? Why or why not? ______________________________
4. Describe how the game Mahjong was an important part of community and Chinese New Year for Chinese immigrant families. ______________________________

Homophone Bingo

Pick eight homophones and write them on your bingo card.

	Free Space	

Letter from the Past Assessment Checklist

Name: ______________________________

Use this chart for self-assessment, peer assessment and teacher evaluation.

	I need more (I haven't included enough yet)	Somewhat (My work lacks some detail)	Yes! (I have met the criteria)
FORM			
Letter Structure			
Flow			
Opening Remarks			
Closing Remarks			
INFORMATION			
Historical Details			
Historical Accuracy			
STYLE			
Word Choice			
Varied Sentences			
Believable Voice			
MECHANICS			
Spelling			
Punctuation			
Grammar			

Chinese New Year: Chapter Three Comprehension Questions

Name: ______________________________

1. How has technology enhanced Chinese New Year celebrations? Give two examples from pages 47–49.

2. How do children show respect to their elders on Chinese New Year? Give two examples.

3. What do the colors red, gold and white symbolize in Chinese culture? Remember to write in complete sentences.

   Red ______________________________

   Gold ______________________________

   White ______________________________

4. Why is giving "lucky money" a symbolic tradition in Chinese culture?

5. What is the core belief of this celebration?

Orca Book Publisher © 2019 Orca Origins Teacher Guide by Tasha Henry • ISBN 9781459822443

Chinese New Year:
Chapter Three Comprehension Questions (cont.)

8. Read Jen's Story (Part One, page 42, and Part Two, page 58). Why do you think Jen's memories of family and the New Year celebrations are tied to cooking and food? How is the preparing and sharing of food a universal symbol of community building? Describe a positive memory that is defined by preparing or sharing food. What did you feel? How is that food forever connected to the memory?

____

____

____

____

9. Read Elaine's Story (pp. 62–63). What contrasts can you identify between Elaine's and Jen's stories? What similarities? What do you think is at stake for families when cultural traditions are not celebrated? Explain your thinking using examples from each story.

____

____

____

____

ORCA TEACHER RESOURCES

Fact Sort Activity

Name: ______________________________

Write down ten true-or-false questions on sticky notes or pieces of paper. Make sure you have five questions for which the answer is true and five questions for which the answer is false. Trade questions with a partner and sort the questions into the true and false columns.

True	False

 • ISBN 9781459822443

Hamsa Amulet Decoration

Color in and cut out the hamsa decoration.

Orca Book Publisher © 2019 Orca Origins Teacher Guide by Tasha Henry • ISBN 9781459822443

ORCA TEACHER RESOURCES

Passover: Comic Storyboard

Name: ______________________________

1

Draw a comic of the Passover story. Write a caption for each picture, explaining the action.

MOSES ASKED THE PHARAOH TO FREE THE ISRAELITES.	

Passover: Comic Storyboard (cont.)

Name: ____________________

2

	ISRAELITES WANDERED IN THE WILDERNESS FOR 40 YEARS

ORCA TEACHER RESOURCES

Seder Meal Symbols

Name: ______________________________

Record the name and meaning for each of the foods found on the seder plate. As you read about the seder meal, think about why it's important for children to be included in the ceremony.

Hebrew Word	Type of Food	What It Symbolizes
Example: beitzah	*Hard-boiled egg*	*The egg offered by ancestors on the altar of the great Temple in Jerusalem at Passover*

 • ISBN 9781459822443

Symbol Poem Writing Activity

Name: ____

Love is (describe smell)

____

____ .

Love is (describe taste)

____

____ .

Love is (name the food in your culture's language)

____

____ .

Passover:
Chapter Two Comprehension Questions

Name: ______________________________

1. Why would it be important for young people to go on The March of the Living?

____

____

____

2. As you read Ben's and Liselotte's stories, what moments struck you as symbolic or profound?

____

____

____

3. Why do you think the writer of this book chose to use memoir as a way to learn about the Holocaust?

____

____

____

4. Choose one photo or picture from this section. In a small group, explain how this picture, for you, captures the message of this chapter.

____

____

____

____

____

5. Pick one quote from this chapter. In a reflection journal, rewrite the quote, including the author's name. What does this quote mean to you? Why are these words significant to the study of the Holocaust and Passover?

____

____

____

____

____

Ramadan: Chapter One Comprehension Questions

Name: ____________________

1. What is a monotheistic religion?

   ____

2. When was Islam created?

   ____

3. Where are the Islamic Holy cities Mecca and Medina located?

   ____

4. What does the word *Islam* mean?

   ____

5. According to Muslims, what are the four key benefits of fasting at Ramadan?

   ____

   ____

   ____

   ____

   ____

6. When does Eid-al-Fitr start?

   ____

   ____

Ramadan:
Fact Sort Activity

Name: ______________________________

Cut out the facts below and sort them into the true and false columns.

True	False

1. Ramadan is one of the pillars of Islam.
2. Ramadan is an opportunity to learn key lessons.
3. There are six pillars in Islam.
4. Christians and Muslims believe in some of the same prophets.
5. All Muslim children fast during Ramadan.
6. Ramadan is always in May.
7. Ramadan is based on the lunar calendar.
8. The Qur'an is a temple where people pray.
9. Taraweeh prayers are special evening prayers in addition to the five daily prayers.
10. Ibtihaj is a Muslim Olympic fencer for the men's American team.

ORCA TEACHER RESOURCES

Ramadan: Chapter Two Comprehension Questions

Name: ______________________________

1. What did the Prophet Muhammad say the three ashras are for? How do Muslims celebrate each of the ashras?

____
____
____
____

2. What is The Night of Destiny?

____
____

3. What is Eid-al-Fitr?

____
____

4. What is the *khutbah*?

____

5. What is the difference between *zakat-al-fitr* and *sadaqa*? Why are they both important to Muslims?

____
____
____
____
____

6. Read the "Ramada Facts" on page 41. Can you think of a community event or family tradition that is similar to Ausma's story of her home on Eid? Discuss with a partner.

____
____
____
____
____

Spirit of Ramadan Research Activity

Name: ______________________________

Complete the chart below with as many details as you can discover. The websites for the organizations are listed on page 83. In the last box, research one of the organizations on page 54–55 or research another Muslim charity organization.

Name of Organization	Where and when did it start?	What does it do?	Who does it help?	An interesting fact
Give 30				
Project Downtown				
Camp Ramadan				

ORCA TEACHER RESOURCES

Ramadan Essay Template

Name: ____

Introduction Paragraph

Around the world, people recognize the Islam tradition of Ramadan. Although some traditions, such as __________________ and __________________, have similarities, some countries celebrate in different ways. I will be contrasting these three countries and the ways in which they celebrate this important Islamic tradition: __________________, __________________ and __________________. The following essay will describe the origins of Islam and the importance of Ramadan for Muslims today, around the world.

First Body Paragraph

Describe the origins of Islam and Ramadan.

Second Body Paragraph

Describe the similarities in the three countries you have chosen to contrast.

Third Body Paragraph

Describe the differences in the three countries you have chosen to contrast.

Conclusion Paragraph

In many parts of the world, such as __________________, __________________ and __________________, Muslims celebrate their religion and beliefs with an important tradition called Ramadan. The main message of this practice is __________________. Although there are similarities and differences in how Ramadan is practiced, the intention, that __________________, is shared by Muslims around the world.

Essay Template

Name: ______________________________

Introduction Paragraph

Around the world, people recognize the traditions of __________________. Although some traditions, such as __________________ and __________________, have similarities, some countries celebrate in different ways. I will be contrasting these three countries and the ways in which they celebrate these traditions: __________________, __________________ and __________________. The following essay will describe the historical origins and the importance of these celebrations today.

First Body Paragraph

Describe the historical origins.

Second Body Paragraph

Describe the similarities in the three countries you have chosen to contrast.

Third Body Paragraph

Describe the differences in the three countries you have chosen to contrast.

Conclusion Paragraph

In many parts of the world, such as __________________, __________________ and __________________, people celebrate their religion and beliefs with important cultural rituals. The main message of these practices are __________________. Although there are similarities and differences in how they are practiced, the intention, that __________________, is shared by people around the world.

ANSWER KEY

Birthdays: Chapter One Comprehension Questions

1. Egyptians
2. Astrology
3. Book of Genesis, New Testament
4. Many babies died in the first week of life
5. Romans/females
6. Artemis, Greek goddess of the moon/moon cakes. It celebrated her radiance
7. Birthdays were seen as pagan or non-Christian.
8. A time of cultural rebirth in Europe between 1300 and 1700 CE
9. A period of time in the mid-1700s defined by invention and technological advances
10. Jawaharlal Nehru was the first prime minister of India, who fought for India's independence from British rule and was an advocate for children's right to education
11. Nelson Mandela

Diwali: Introduction Comprehension Questions

1. Light row
2. A monotheistic religion only believes in one god
3. No, because Hinduism has millions of gods and goddesses
4. Yes, because Sikhism only has one god
5. Lakshmi
6. She loves Diwali and was excited to share the festival with other people. She felt like Lakshmi was shining a light on her

ANSWER KEY

Birthdays: Birthday Traditions Around the World

COUNTRY OR REGION	TYPES OF FOOD	ACTIVITIES/RITUALS
United States—Winnebago tribe	• Sheet cakes	• A huge party • Drumming and singing • Playing a game where you guess where a bone or stone is hidden
Nigeria	• A whole goat • Jollof rice	• A huge party
Germany	• *Geburtstagstorten*	• Putting candles on birthday cakes • Lighting a Lebenskerze until you turn 12 • Putting coins in the cake
Egypt	• Two cakes • Small individual cakes • Sesame sticks • Little sandwiches	• Turning 7 is special because you go from being a kid to being school age • Girls wear a tiara and fancy dress • They get candy from a pabitin
Philippines	• Birthday cake • Jaz • Pancit • *Lechon, adobo*	• Presents are wrapped in brightly colored paper • The birthday kid wears fancy clothing • Touching your parents' feet to show respect
Norway	• Ice cream	• Playing a game where you hang frozen treats from strings and fish for them
India	• Spicy curry • Chutney • *Dudh pakh*	• Presents are wrapped in brightly colored paper • The birthday kid wears fancy clothing • Touching your parents' feet to show respect
Ecuador	• Raisin cake • Tea cookies • Hot chocolate	• Celebrating their saint's day with an afternoon tea party
Israel	• Cake shaped like the birthday child's special interest	• Wearing a crown of leaves or flowers • Sitting in a chair decorated with streamers, which guests dance around while singing • Playing games like racing with a hard-boiled egg on a spoon

ORCA TEACHER RESOURCES

ANSWER KEY

Diwali: Chapter Two Comprehension Questions

1. The Chinese
2. A law that prohibited Asian people from entering the United States
3. Others
4. The immigration and nationality act of 1965 removed barriers for immigrants
5. Sikhs, in 1903
6. They were called Hindus
7. Filled-in timeline:

Year	Description of incident, act or policy in Canada
1897	Hundreds of troops from across the British Empire were brought to London to celebrate Queen Victoria's Diamond Jubilee, and the Sikh regiment from India was brought back to British India by traveling through Canada.
1903	The first immigrants from India arrived in British Columbia to escape famine and pandemics in India.
1906	Influx of immigrants to the cities of Victoria and Vancouver. The new Immigration Act was passed.
1907	A law was passed that restricted Chinese, Japanese and Indian people from voting, and all immigrants from Asia were stripped of their citizenship.
1908	Canadian officials met with leaders of the Indian community and proposed that immigrants accept indentured labor in the West Indies.
1913	Thirty-nine Sikhs arrived in Victoria via Hong Kong and were detained.
1914	The Komagata Maru arrived in Calcutta, and the British killed twenty people.
2016	Prime Minister Justin Trudeau apologized in the House of Commons for the Komagata Maru incident.

8. Answers will vary
9. Answers will vary

ANSWER KEY

Christmas: Chapter One Comprehension Questions

1. Answers will vary
2. December 21 or 22
3. Ancient peoples would await the longer days, hence a midwinter celebration
4. It was burned through the night, and the ashes would be put out on the fields to fertilize crops
5. Any logical analysis—human need for connection, warmth, food in the darkest or coldest months
6. A festival for Saturn, god of seeds and prosperity, celebrating fertility and crops with an exchange of gifts and candles
7. A festival of Dionysus, god of song and dance
8. In the Middle Ages in Europe, workers asked for tips in a box the day after Christmas. Answers about interpretations will vary

Christmas: Matching Activity

1. Sinterklaas
2. Magi
3. Crèche
4. Myrrh
5. Christianity
6. St. Nicholas
7. Sol Invictus
8. Fourth century in Rome
9. St. Hilary of Poitiers
10. New Testament
11. Christmas
12. 12 days of Christmas
13. BCE
14. Advent wreath
15. Puritans

ORCA TEACHER RESOURCES

ANSWER KEY

Midwinter Traditions Scavenger Hunt

Traditions	Place	Drawing or Description
Yule Logs and the Yule Goat	• France • Scandinavia	
Boxing Day	• Canada • Commonwealth Countries	
Flying Chariots	• Ancient Greece • Scandinavia • India	
Christmas Carols	• Egyptians • Greeks • Romans • Celts	
Saint Nicholas	• Europe	

TEACHER RESOURCES

ANSWER KEY

Chinese New Year: Chapter One Comprehension Questions

1. Lunar New Year and Spring Festival
2. The Nián is a mythical beast that brings illness and bad luck but is scared of bright colors and loud noises.
3. The Jade Emperor wanted to measure the passage of time, so he set up a race across a river. The years are named after the twelve animals that crossed the finish line. Answers will vary.
4. Chinese immigrants organized Mahjong tournaments at which they were able to make friends.

Chinese New Year: Chapter Three Comprehension Questions

1. New Year celebrations in recent years have included laser light shows, Chinese-language hip-hop musicians performing alongside traditional Chinese opera singers, parades being live-streamed on the Internet, red lucky money being sent and received with messaging apps, and computer-designed firework displays. Answers will vary.
2. Children show respect to their elders on Chinese New Year by visiting; bringing gifts of fruit, candy and lucky money; helping prepare the big dinner, creating decorations and banners; and helping set off the firecrackers.
3. Red is associated with fire and also with happy and exciting celebrations.
   Gold is the color of wealth and nobility and is used to welcome in a year of prosperity.
   White is the color of sadness and bad luck.
4. Giving "lucky money" is a symbolic tradition in Chinese culture that represents maintaining happiness and health and keeping your family safe.
5. The core belief of this celebration is the hope that our loved ones will be healthy and happy during the coming year and for many years to come.
6. Answers will vary.
7. Answers will vary.

ORCA TEACHER RESOURCES

ANSWER KEY

Passover: Comic Storyboard

Answers may vary, but key events should be similar to these.
Panels should appear in this sequence.

1. Moses asked the pharaoh to free the Israelites.
2. The pharaoh refused.
3. God punished the pharaoh by sending a series of plagues.
4. The pharaoh still refused.
5. God sent the Angel of Death to kill the firstborn of every family.
6. God warned the Israelites to mark their doors so the Angel of Death would pass over them.
7. The pharaoh agreed to free the Israelites.
8. The Israelites had to leave immediately.
9. The pharaoh changed his mind and sent his soldiers after the Israelites.
10. The Red Sea parted and the Israelites were able to cross safely.
11. The soldiers tried to follow, but the Red Sea came crashing back, and they drowned.
12. Israelites wandered in the wilderness for 40 years.

Seder Meal Symbols

Hebrew Word	Type of Food	What It Symbolizes
Example: beitzah	Hard-boiled egg	The egg offered by ancestors on the altar of the great Temple in Jerusalem at Passover
paschal	Roasted shank bone	The lamb sacrificed by ancestors and offered on the altar of the great Temple in Jerusalem at Passover
maror	Horseradish	The bitterness of slavery
hazeret	Romaine lettuce	The bitterness of slavery
charoset	Paste made from fruit and nuts	The mortar ancestors used to make bricks when they were slaves in Egypt
karpas	Parsley or celery dipped in salt water	The arrival of spring

Orca Book Publisher © 2019 Orca Origins Teacher Guide by Tasha Henry • ISBN 9781459822443

ANSWER KEY

Passover: Chapter Two Comprehension Questions

1. It is important for young people to go to on The March of the Living so they can learn about the Holocaust and what people went through.
2. Answers will vary.
3. Answers will vary.
4. Answers will vary.
5. Answers will vary.

Ramadan: Chapter One Comprehension Questions

1. A religion with one god
2. 610 CE
3. Saudi Arabia
4. Submission and peace
5. Becoming recharged in all areas of your life; feeling empathy for those less fortunate; strengthening a sense of community; reaffirming the belief that all human beings are equal
6. The new moon at the end of Ramadan

Ramadan: Fact Sort Activity

1. True
2. True
3. False
4. True
5. False
6. False
7. True
8. False
9. True
10. False

ANSWER KEY

Ramadan: Chapter Two Comprehension Questions

1. The first ashra is for mercy and is a time when Muslims reflect on whether they have been good people and apologize for committing acts that are forbidden to Muslims. The second ashra is for forgiveness and is a time when Muslims show mercy to others and forgive them when they apologize. The third ashra is for salvation and is a time when Muslims pray, do good deeds and self-reflect.
2. The Night of Destiny is one of the last odd-number nights of Ramadan and is the holiest night of the year.
3. Eid-al-Fitr is the end of Ramadan and the Festival of Breaking the Fast.
4. The *khutbah* was the last sermon given by the Prophet Muhammad.
5. *Zakat-al-fitr* is a small donation that all Muslims must make on Eid day based on their needs. *Sadaqa* is a voluntary form of giving that Muslims may participate in at any time of the year. Zakat-al-fitr and Sadaqa are important to Muslims because charity and acts of service for the benefit of others are an essential part of the Islamic faith.
6. Answers will vary.

Spirit of Ramadan Research Activity

Name of Organization	Where and when did it start?	What does it do?	Who does it help?	An interesting fact
Give 30	• Canada • 2012	• Donates to food banks	• The hungry	• Answers will vary
Project Downtown	• Miami, FL • 2006	• Donates food • Donates clothes • Donates toiletries	• The homeless • The hungry	• Answers will vary
Camp Ramadan	• Washington, DC • 2013	• Runs a summer day camp for Muslim children	• Muslim children who feel pressured to be ambassadors for their faith	• Answers will vary
Organization will vary	• Answers will vary	• Answers will vary	• Answers will vary	• Answers will vary